No More Back Pain

By Alan Chisholm

I0143144

The Practical Guide to Living a Happier, Healthier and More Productive Life

NO MORE BACK PAIN

Copyright © 2015 by Alan Chisholm

To Dad, Mum, Jess, Lucy, Branco, Stevie, Mick UTV,
The Wrestling Crew and The Civic Drive Boys

Thanks for all your help

Contents

Introduction.. 7
Part 1: All your muscles are connected........... 13
Part 2: Biological Maintenance..................... 15
    - Electrolytes and Muscle Cramps.......... 16
    - Magnesium.. 17
    - Calcium, Sodium & Potassium........... 18
Part 3: Physical Maintenance...................... 23
    - Dynamic Stretching......................... 25
    - Static Stretching............................. 41
Part 4: When You're In Pain...................... 53
    - Lower back/hips.............................. 53
    - Neck.. 59
Part 5: Long-term Maintenance................... 61
    - Strengthening Exercises................... 61
    - In the gym..................................... 65
    - Squats, Deadlifts and Upright Rows.... 68
Part 6: The Other Stuff............................. 69
    - Orthotics....................................... 69
    - Painkillers, Creams and Ointments..... 70
    - Foam Roller................................... 71
Part 7: Dos and Don'ts............................. 77
References... 78

Introduction

Wow.

I can't believe it.

As I'm writing this, I'm actually smiling.

For the first time in years, I'm free of back pain.

I've just finished playing a basketball game – 40 minutes worth of jumping, running, stopping, starting – and I'm confident I'm going to be able to walk tomorrow. My back isn't cramped, my hips don't feel like they're going to cave in on each other, and I'll actually be able to get a good night's sleep.

But the funny thing is… 3 years ago I was ready to kill myself. Literally ready to kill myself. I saw a car coming at me, and I thought, if I step in front of it, I won't have to put up with this pain anymore.

A bit over the top I know, but that's exactly the way I felt. And after thinking that, that's when I broke down; I collapsed on the side of an SUV by the side of the road, and I cried, and I cried, and I cried… all because I didn't have a solution. I had just been to my local GP, and he told me there was nothing wrong with me. The x-rays were fine, nothing was out of place, so therefore I shouldn't be feeling any pain whatsoever.

"It's probably just all in your head," said the Doc, and they were the words that crushed me. Worried that I would do something that would affect my family and friends for the rest of their lives, I took myself to the emergency room, where I lay on the floor of the waiting room for about two hours. Luckily, I managed to pull myself together and get some support.

But this wasn't the result of something that could be fixed with a few panadols or a week's rest. This was ongoing, constant back pain.

Up until that point, the pain through my hips and lower spine had lasted for two years. Two years of struggling to get out of bed in the morning, not knowing why these aches were there and wondering why they weren't going away. All the muscles under my waist were constantly cramped, robbing me of any comfort whatsoever throughout the day. It was hell, every day, and it all became too much.

Now don't confuse this for a sob story. Leading up to my injury, I felt I could do anything. I'd just won a gold medal in tae-kwon-do at the University games, I managed to score myself a half-decent looking girlfriend, and I was very much pain free. At that point, I would say I was on top of the world. But then, through a lack of knowledge of how to take care of my body, everything came crumbling down.

After a normal game of basketball, I was on the ground. Everything was seizing up, right from my lower tailbone to the top of my spine, and I didn't know what to do. I lay there, scared, but was still confident that this was just your average injury, and it would all get better in a week's time. But it didn't get better… it only got worse. Sure I could walk again, but only with painkillers, and after a month or two, I became addicted to them. It wasn't long before I'd used up all my sick days at work, so I had to apply for a disability allowance from the government. And that's when the downward spiral began. I had to drink lots of coffee to combat the drowsiness from the painkillers, but then my mood began to fluctuate as a side effect. Then I had to take a heartburn mixture to compensate for the stomach cramps induced by the painkillers. Then I had to take diarrhea tablets to fix the bowel problems from the heartburn medication. Then I went cold turkey on everything because I didn't like where this was going. And that's when I felt like I was losing my mind.

I had no choice; I had to go back on the painkillers – I needed them. The pain was constant. I couldn't sit down, I couldn't drive, I couldn't sleep… the only time the pain wasn't there was when I lay on my side. But that's great if you live in a world where you don't have to eat, work or satisfy your woman… who I would end up losing. She said it wasn't because of the injury, but I know that we would've lasted a lot longer if I hadn't turned into a sad wreck of a man.

I wasn't being stupid about things though.

I wasn't just getting drugged up and spending my days moping about. I was actively seeking help, seeing chiropractors, osteopaths, physiotherapists, but none of them could help. They twisted me, massaged me, manipulated me, but after a few days following the treatment, the pain persisted. And I don't care who you are, that will break you. Mentally, physically, emotionally… the whole deal. You just give up, no matter how many times you listen to Eminem's 'Lose Yourself', or how many times you hear "She'll be right mate!" (Australian for all will be fine).

I thought I was done for, and was accepting that this was life from now on, but then I crossed paths with a tall Yugoslavian man named Branco. We didn't fall in love, but I was very close after the treatment and advice he gave me. He was working as a remedial masseuse at my local leisure centre, and he told me one thing that fixed my back problems for good.

And it was so damn simple.

Did he touch my back? Massage it in any way? No.

He told me I have short hamstrings, and I needed to stretch them at least twice a day. He enforced that *one hundred percent* of back pain can be traced down to the legs – something I hadn't even considered - and sure enough, after only a month of stretching my legs twice a day, my back pain was cured.

Over, finito, gone, and I had my life back again.

I could sit down without any pain, I could drive a car, I could go to the nightclub and attempt to dance… it was such a relief I felt like crying. Actually, I think I did.

After this change came about, I was ecstatic. The feeling was pure euphoria – it was like I'd stumbled upon this miracle cure, one that was under my nose but had eluded me the entire time.

But perhaps equally, if not more, I felt frustration.

Absolute, sheer *frustration*.

Why did it take me two years of depression, pain and near suicide to solve this problem? Why had I already spent upwards of $2000 dollars on treatments, creams, x-rays, MRIs and pain removal machines that shocked my muscles into responding?

Why had everyone else I'd seen – the chiropractors, the physiotherapists, the osteopaths – fixed me for a day or so, but after the treatment wore off, I was back to square one, ready to spend more money on another temporary fix.

So much time… wasted. I was furious.

Don't get me wrong, these back specialists aren't

incompetent. They know the muscles, joints and ligaments – everything that one needs to know in order to treat the body – but do they really stress what's important? Do they leave you with a detailed set of tools that will help you for the rest of your days? Some might, but from my experience, the answer is no. What I find they give you, unintentionally or not, are temporary fixes. The men and women I visited didn't stress the changes I needed to make to keep me away from them forever, so I decided to pursue what I needed to know so I wouldn't end up back there.

Over the last few years, I have become obsessed with researching and trialing the best ways to combat back pain. Since I started implementing these measures, my overall quality of life has improved and I've barely needed to visit any kind of practitioner. The aim of this book, put simply, is to eliminate the need for those temporary fixes so you won't have to spend any more money on them. The only person you're going to rely on is yourself, and with that little bit of effort each day, you can build a body that you will be in control of... not the other way round.

Part 1: All your muscles are connected.

Okay, here's an important point to consider: all your muscles are connected.

They're not connected in the sense that they're touching one other, but they *are* connected like carriages on a train are connected.

If one goes, the whole system is disrupted.

Whenever a certain muscle, or a group of muscles, have suffered a strain or injury, other muscles in the body will compensate by working harder in an attempt to bring the body back into balance. This process is known as muscular compensation, and if left untreated for too long, serious injuries can result[1]. So in order to keep the muscular system functioning at an optimum level, you have to give your time, effort and care to each component, and this can be achieved in two ways:

1. Biological maintenance and
2. Physical maintenance

I choose the word maintenance very carefully, because you must understand that this is an ongoing process. There is no once off solution to fixing back pain; it requires daily attention and constant care. But don't be dismayed by this idea of constant effort. The more often you do it, the easier it will become. A simpler way of understanding this is by using an analogy with a sink full of dishes. If you leave them alone for a while, they will build up until you have to set aside a stupid amount of time in your day to get the job done. But if you wash the dishes every day, it will barely seem like you've made an effort at all, and you'll still end up with a clean sink.

The reasoning behind this idea is that the body is dynamic, which means it's in a state of constant change. Depending on what you choose to do throughout the day, your skeletal system and muscular system will adjust to suit your behaviours, usually at the detriment of your day-to-day comfort[2]. For example, you might see a boy who has played video games for extensive periods of time with a hunched over back, or a mother who has carried her children on her hip with a slight bend to her posture.

Ideally, you don't want a skeletal or muscular system that has been warped or shaped in any way. You want the shape of your muscles to give you a high degree of flexibility, and you don't want your skeletal system to be modified to suit any kind of lazy behaviour. Unless you've suffered a life-changing injury, this level of flexibility can be achieved by acquiring knowledge of the two points above: biological and physical maintenance.

Whether it be the personal trainer at your gym or a YouTube video on stretching from a reliable source, there are thousands of resources available that discuss ways to alleviate back pain, but from what I've seen, they all seem to miss one very important thing: the order and time in which you must do things.

Pay close attention to the following chapters. You will learn how to eliminate back pain, live a happier life and escape the merry-go-round of doctors, specialists and a depressing collection of receipts.

Part 2: Biological Maintenance

After my experience with back pain, I've found that creating an internal environment that will assist all the efforts you make to reduce your pain is so important. What this means, is that there is no point in stretching, exercising or correcting your posture if your muscles are going to revert back to a previously worse state. Your diet and nutrition will determine how well your body responds to external changes, so you want to make sure these are taken care of to the best extent

So before we look into the physical side of things, let's talk about back pain in the context of the *biological processes* of the body (i.e. the chemical reactions taking place in your body's systems every moment of the day). By gaining this understanding, you will lay a foundation that will allow you to perform stretches and exercises that will be effective and long-lasting.

Muscle cramps occur due to number of reasons [2]. The most common are:
- they're not accustom to demands of a certain exercise.
- they've been overworked.
- they're dehydrated, and the body is lacking electrolytes.

These first two points are quite simple to control.
If we haven't done a certain exercise before, or we haven't reached a particular level of fitness, we shouldn't attempt something that is beyond our current physical capacity. But the third point... well there's an area where we can really make a difference.
On any regular day, we can go hours without drinking

water or consuming food that contains any of the main electrolytes. At this point, we could go into a whole lot of scientific jargon that explains the chemical pathways that lead to muscle cramping, but unless you've got dreams of lecturing university students, or developing synthetic powders to sell to sports nutrition companies, you're probably not going to find that very useful.

The main idea is to stay hydrated.

In order to reduce the likelihood of muscle cramps and soreness, you should be consuming the recommended daily intake of water - **3.4 L/day for men and 2.8 L/day for women**[3] - and finding a way to get those electrolytes in your system. Personally, I buy a tub of one of the something-or-other 'ade' drinks from the supermarkets (which is far cheaper than buying individual bottles), and mixing myself one or two servings a day. However, since these sports drinks can have a relatively high sugar content, a lot of people are adverse to including them in their regular diet. But that's okay, because there are plenty of foods with high levels of electrolytes that are far cheaper than takeaway alternatives. The following sections contain all the information you need on electrolytes in regards to back pain:

Electrolytes and Muscle Cramps

In terms of overcoming back pain, a sound knowledge of electrolytes is important as these molecules play a vital role in nerve and muscle function. You do not need to understand the precise nature of chemical reactions, just the fact that there are four electrolytes – **magnesium,**

calcium, sodium and potassium – that will assist your body in maintaining proper muscle function. [1]

When it comes to tackling discomfort through the back, it's likely that you'll be focused on the physical side of things (i.e. making expensive appointments to receive treatments), but neglecting the internal, biological component. As mentioned before, there is no point in receiving treatment for your back if your body is just going to revert back to the same state a few days later. You are spending a lot of money for a temporary fix. Ideally, you want create an internal environment that will allow your muscles to heal quickly and reduce the likelihood of cramping. So instead of looking solely towards massages, acupuncture and other physical treatment, firstly turn your attention to what is going on inside your body, because this is what controls the way muscles function. Here are some good points about electrolytes to remember:

Magnesium

Magnesium is often referred to as the miracle mineral. Why? Because it plays an important role in many chemical pathways integral to good health, such as those associated with energy production, nerve impulses, muscular contractions and regular heart rhythm[3]. In regards to eliminating back pain, meeting your recommended daily intake (RDI) levels of magnesium will be beneficial to you in a number of ways, particularly by reducing the likelihood of muscle cramps and the chance that your muscles will revert to an uncomfortable state[2]. Magnesium can be found in a variety of food or purchased from supermarkets as a supplement.

RDI
Adults: 300 – 400mg a day
Children (9-13 years): 200mg a day. [3]

Good Food Sources
Green leafy vegetables (particularly spinach), legumes, peanuts, cashews, almonds, cereal (shredded wheat), wholemeal bread, soymilk, peanut butter, avocado, rice, yoghurt, oatmeal, banana, salmon and milk.[3]

Calcium, Sodium and Potassium

Muscle contraction is dependent upon the presence of these three electrolytes[2], and that's basically all you need to know. Feel free to research the chemical pathways involved in the reactions, however that information isn't really going to assist your back pain and is superfluous in regards to your recovery. The question to ask yourself now is:

Am I deficient in any of these electrolytes?

If the answer turns out to be yes, then you are more likely to experience muscle weakness and severe contractions than someone who is meeting their RDIs[2]. See the following tables for all the information you need in regards to maintaining your capacity for proper muscle function.
Something else to keep in mind is that the balances between electrolytes, in particular sodium and potassium,

are essential when it comes to the regulation of fluids in your body[3]. And since muscle cramps are associated with dehydration, or the rapid loss of water in the body, it is very importance that these gradients are maintained[2, 3]. This is also the reason why, if you look on the backs of sports drinks, you will see sodium and potassium as the main ingredients (apart from sugar of course). By replenishing the electrolytes you lose during exercise, these drinks are effectively restoring the osmotic gradients that regulate the hydration of the body. As a general rule, you should always look to eat foods or take supplements that contain electrolytes directly after exercising. Here is some info on electrolytes published by the National Health and Medical Research Council of Australia (NHMRC).

	Calcium
Adult RDI	840 mg/day
Children (9-13) RDI	800 mg/day
Good Food Sources	Yoghurt, cheese, sardines, milk, soymilk, orange juice, salmon, tofu, kale, bread, legumes, nuts, breakfast cereals.

	Sodium*
Adult RDI	460-920 mg/day
Children (9-13) RDI	400-800 mg/day
Good Food Sources	Crab, pickles, cucumber, olives, green leafy vegetables, cereals (shredded wheat and bran), celery.

	Potassium
Adult RDI	3800 mg/day
Children (9-13) RDI	2500 - 3000 mg/day
Good Food Sources	Green, leafy vegetables, fruit from vines (grapes and blackberries), root vegetables (carrots and potatoes), citrus fruits such as oranges and grapefruits, beans, dried apricot, avocados, mushrooms, bananas, fish, squash, yoghurt

BE CAREFUL!

Any nutrient can be detrimental to your health if taken in excess, but **sodium/salt** is one that should be monitored very closely. According to the NHMRC, high levels of sodium in your diet may put you at risk of high blood pressure, a stroke, heart failure, osteoporosis, stomach cancer, kidney disease, kidney stones, headaches and an enlarged heart. Foods you should avoid eating, or eat occasionally are: table salt, processed cheese, salad dressings, margarine, processed meat, pancake mix, pizza hut, Asian sauces, instant soups and... caviar (you may have to dig deep to give up that one).

You may have noticed there is an abundance of healthy, natural foods on the lists of food sources above. Considering we humans have adapted to the natural environment around us, it is no surprise that there are little to no processed foods on the lists. Processed foods, in particular take-away foods, are manufactured specifically for taste, and generally not beneficial for your overall health and life expectancy. Therefore, if you include a selection of the foods in the table above in your weekly shopping list, you may find yourself feeling a lot better and saving a lot of money on your food bill each week!

In addition to a healthy diet, I recommend taking a multi-vitamin every day to ensure the body has an adequate supply of trace elements to carry out all the important chemical reactions.

Part 3: Physical Maintenance

As mentioned before, I've been told that 100% of pain in the back relates to the flexibility of your legs. This exact figure may not be purported in studies, however studies *have* shown that a lack of hamstring flexibility is strongly correlated to subjects with a history of lower back pain[4]. What I'd like to point out, is that this was the ONLY advice that made a real difference in my life, ultimately getting me off painkillers and government disability payments. I mean sure, it was great not having to go to work, but I'd choose to have a good back any day of the week. So now I'd encourage you to pay close attention to everything in this chapter, because there's a good chance it will work for you as well.

In terms of back pain in general, you may *feel* it your back, but the likely source is the tight muscles that are pulling down from below. For example, if your calve muscles are tight, your hamstrings are going to feel the strain, which will in turn pull down on your lower back, which will in turn pull down on your upper back, which will in turn pull down on your neck. And it's usually at that point where you'll be calling in sick to work, slumping on your bed or popping a few painkillers just to make it through the day. The solution: you must change the shape of your muscles, because too much movement without maintenance will reduce your flexibility and leave you susceptible to cramping[1]. This train of thought certainly isn't new (the study referenced in the previous sentence is from 1992), but it was only stressed to me *after two years* of searching for a solution.

Just to drive the point home, back pain has everything to do with the fact your muscles are connected and the whole system relies on each and every one playing their part. Obviously this doesn't apply to every person; some people have suffered a serious accident or have a condition like scoliosis that changes the shape of their spine, but in general, we are all the same. We have the same basic skeletal structure and those dangly things coming from hips play the most significant role.
This section provides a range of stretches that will help relieve all the tension that transfers from these areas, ultimately allowing you to go about your day pain free. Important: pay attention to the order in which you should do things and at what part of your day.

** SOME GROUND RULES **

1. Do not cause yourself pain. Stretching can exacerbate injuries if you push yourself too hard. Relax and take it slow.
2. Be patient. Let your flexibility improve gradually over time.
3. Consistent, daily effort gets results.
4. Stretch on a soft or cushioned surface, such a gym mat, yoga mat or the carpet.
5. Always consider your medical history. If you have suffered any serious injuries to your back, or have any conditions that affect your skeletal, muscular or nervous systems, consult with your doctor before attempting any of these stretches.
6. Don't put yourself at risk. If you are unsure about any exercises, consult a personal trainer at your local gym.

DYNAMIC STRETCHING

Dynamic stretches are stretches where the body is in motion, and should be employed for muscles that haven't been warmed up yet. Basically, dynamic stretching is used in situations where you haven't been moving for a long time, such as when you wake up in the morning, when you've been sitting down for a long time, or for your warm up at the gym. As shown in a number of studies, dynamic stretching is more effective than static stretching (stretches that require no movement) when it comes to preparing your body for exercise and reducing injury in the gym [5, 6, 7].

Dynamic stretching only takes up 10 minutes of your day, but it can make all the difference when it comes to alleviating back pain. The following diagrams depict the stretches that you will benefit from, and should be performed every day. As mentioned before – your muscles are dynamic and will shape in accordance with what they are made to do, or to put it better, what they are not made to do.

Therefore, there is no set period to this dynamic stretching plan; I recommend that you perform these exercises every day for the rest of your life.

Improving your flexibility should now become one of your main priorities, whereby you dedicate at least ten minutes a day to stretching your muscles. This requires willpower and regular effort, but the result is less pain and a happier life.

The important part is to be patient. Stretching doesn't need to be painful; it will be most successful when you seek to make a little bit of progress during each successive stretching session. Remember: this is a process. You may not be fully relieved of your pain after the first session or two, but if you are consistent and do not give up, you will eventually become more flexible and the pain will go away. The following dynamic stretches should be performed in the order in which they are presented.

The Shin Runner

(Calves, hamstrings, lower back)

- The perfect way to start the day.

Step 1. Stand up straight, lean over and don't bend your knees.

Step 2. Start with your finger tips on your knees, then run them down your shins as far as you can.

Step 3. Run your fingers back up to the starting position. Perform 20 times.

The Toe Touch

(Calves, hamstrings, lower back)

- Advanced form of The Shin Runner.

Instead of going from knees to shins, you are going from your knees to your toes. After 2-3 months of performing this exercise every day, you should be able to touch your toes.

The Washing Machine

(Upper back, lower back, shoulders, obliques)

- Loosens up all the muscles running up and down your spine.

Step 1. Stand straight with your arms extended at right angles to your body, fingers stretched out and feet facing forward.

Step 2. Twist side to side, allowing your arms to move freely and your muscles to loosen up. Keep your feet facing forward and do not cause yourself any pain. You may hear cricks and cracks through your back, but this is just air trapped in joints[2]. Repeat 10-15 times each side.

The Rainbow
(Obliques and latissimus dorsi)

- Loosen up those tight sides.

Step 1. Stand up straight with your feet a little further than shoulder-width apart.

Step 2. Raise your right hand above your head, then allow your body to fall down to your left hand side.

Step 3. Raise your hand back up to the starting position, effectively moving it in the shape of the rainbow. Repeat 15-20 times. You can then raise you left arm and perform on your right hand side.

The Flamingo
(Quadriceps, abductors)

- A subtle stretch that will alleviate tightness through the front.

Step 1. Stand up straight, grab your right ankle and bring your heel to your right glute. Hold a wall for balance.
Step 2. Keeping your core strong, allow your right knee to swing back and forth. Your ankle is allowed to move off your glute for this one, and make sure to keep your hips/pelvis straight and flat.
Step 3. Repeat 15-20 times, then move onto other leg.

The Kick-Up
(Hamstrings, calves, achilles)

- The Holy Grail. Seriously.

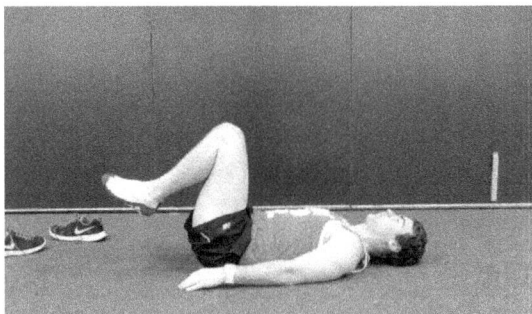

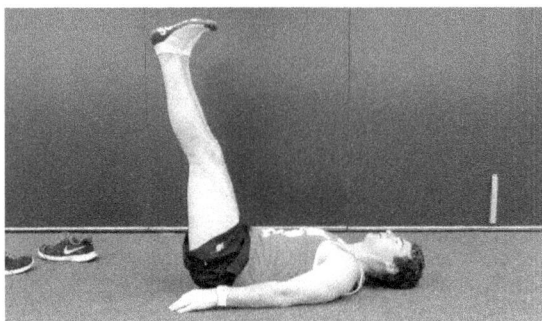

Step 1. Lie on your back with your feet off the ground, thighs 90 degrees to the floor.

Step 2. Keeping your thighs in the same position and your knees still, extend your feet upwards. TOES MUST BE PULLED BACK TOWARDS THE KNEE AT ALL TIMES.

Step 3. Keep the knee still and lower your feet down to the starting position. Repeat 15-20 times.

The Frog Kick

(Hamstrings, calves, achilles)

- Might want to close the bedroom door for this one

Step 1. Lie on your back with your feet off the ground, thighs 90 degrees apart.

Step 2. Keeping your thighs in the same position and your knees still, extend your feet out as if you were doing a frog kick. TOES MUST BE PULLED BACK TOWARDS THE KNEE AT ALL TIMES.

Step 3. Keep the knee still and lower your feet down to the starting position. Repeat 15-20 times.

The Flying V
(Hamstrings, calves)

- Great for the hips and lower back. You may only get a few centimeters of motion, but very effective.

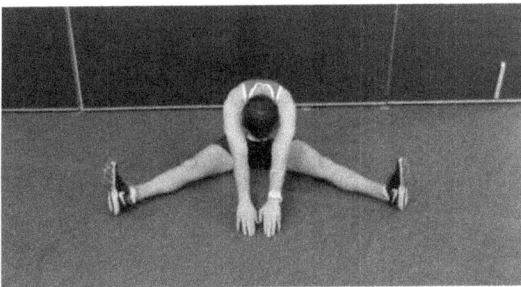

Step 1. Sit on the floor with your legs stretched out in front of you and at 90 degrees apart.

Step 2. Reach your hands out to the floor as far as you can without causing yourself any pain.

Step 3. While angling your toes back towards your head, move your hands back and forth along the floor so you feel a stretch in your hamstrings and calves. Repeat 15-20 times.

The Pelvic Hip Thrust

(Abdominals, quadriceps)

- Again, close the bedroom door…

This move is particularly beneficial if you've been sitting down for long periods of time, because it counteracts the forward pulling force that has been exerted on your hips.

Step 1. Lie on your back with your knees raised and hands by your side.
Step 2. Thrust your pelvis into the air and then lower your back down to the floor.
Step 3. Repeat 15-20 times.

Inside Insides

(Obliques, glutes, erector spinae)

This dynamic stretch will help to loosen the muscles that like to cramp up around your tailbone, which can cause you pain when you're sitting or lying down.

Step 1. Start by lying on your back, knees raised and arms flat by your sides.

Step 2. Spread your feet slightly further than shoulder-width apart and angle your knees inwards.

Step 3. Swing your right knee down to your left ankle, then swing your left knee down to your right ankle. Repeat 15 -20 times.

The Godsend

- The best dynamic stretch in existence. Instant results.

Step 1. Hang off a beam with your hands shoulder-width apart and feet off the floor.
Step 2. While keep your body still, move your legs in alternate directions back and forth. It doesn't matter which leg go first, but just keep your toes curled upwards so you can maximize the calf/hamstring stretch.
Step 3. When one leg moves back and forth, that is 1 rep. Perform15-20 reps.

STATIC STRETCHING

Static stretching differs from dynamic stretching in the sense that there is no movement involved and the stretches are performed as a cool down or recovery, not a warm up.

Important: Do not perform static stretching before exercise. Studies have shown that performing static stretching before exercise will actually increase your risk of injury[8]. But also, numerous studies have shown static stretching to be more effective than dynamic stretching when it comes to improving the flexibility of your muscles[9,10,11].

Again, like dynamic stretching, it should never be painful. You should stay within your pain limits and try to gradually increase your flexibility over time. Muscles can be stubborn, but if stretching is regular and consistent (i.e. 2-3 times per day, every day), they will eventually lengthen and allow you more movement. **Static stretching should only be performed after exercise and before going to bed at night.** Try and perform these stretches in the order in which they're presented.

The Single Leg Toe Touch

(Hamstrings, calves, lower back)

If you can't touch your toes (and let's be honest, most of us can't) grab an area of your shin that stretches your muscle but doesn't cause you pain. Keep toes pointed backwards to maximise the stretch.

Step 1. Sit cross-legged and then extend one out in front of your body, keeping the opposite foot at the knee.
Step 2. While pressing your leg flat on the floor, reach forwards and grab onto your toe.
Step 3. Hold for 30-45 seconds, then repeat on opposite leg.

The Flying V Hold

(Hamstrings, calves, lower back)

- Same as The Flying V, but static.

Sit on the floor, extend legs out in front of you at 90 degree angle and reach forward as far as you can without hurting yourself. Hold for 30-45 seconds and angle those toes back.

The Double Leg Toe Touch
(Hamstrings, calves, lower back)

- Advanced form of the single leg because it's much harder to do.

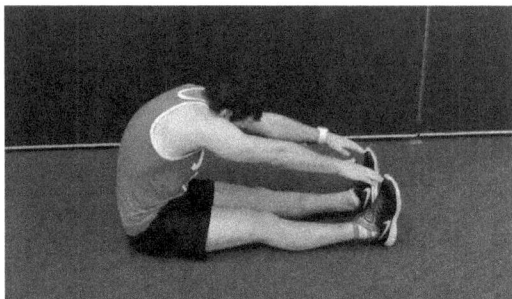

Step 1. Sit down, stretch your legs out in front of you and touch your toes.
Step 2. Bear down and hold for 30-45 seconds

If you can't touch your toes, find an area of your shin that you're comfortable with and keep your toes pointed back.

The Glute Crossover

(Gluteus maximus)

- Stretching your glutes will relieve tightness through the hips and lower back.

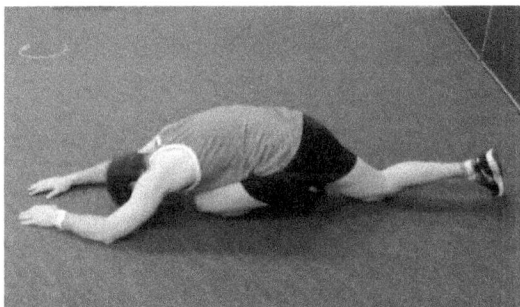

Step 1. Start by placing yourself on all fours, then bring your left leg under your stomach/chest so that your left heel is in front of your right knee.
Step 2. Relax the rest of your body and allow yourself to fall into your leg so that you feel a good stretch through your thigh and glute. Keep square.
Step 3. Hold for 30-45 seconds, repeat on the other side.

The Crouching Tiger

(Hamstrings, glutes)

- One of the best stretches to relieve the tension through your hips and lower back, but probably one to do away from the public eye.

Step 1. Start with feet a little further than shoulder width apart.
Step 2. Squat down with your elbows on the insides of your knees, keeping your back straight the entire time. Hold for 30-45 seconds, using to elbows to gently push outwards and increase the stretch.

The Quad Pull

(Quadriceps)

- The most effective stretch I've found for the quadriceps.
With this position you can locate the areas of tightness
and feel them disappear.

Step 1. Lie face down with your left arm and left leg
extended, but your right arm and right leg bent at 90°.
Step 2. Use your right hand to grab your left ankle of
your opposite leg.
Step 3. Relaxing the rest of your body, pull your ankle
into your glute, flattening your quadriceps on the floor
and stretching the muscle. Hold for 30-45 seconds, then
repeat on the opposite side.

The Cobra
(Abdominals)

This stretch is particularly good for relieving back pain after you've been sitting down for long periods of time. By pushing you pelvis into the floor, you are counteracting the forces that cause you to slouch and adopt back posture.

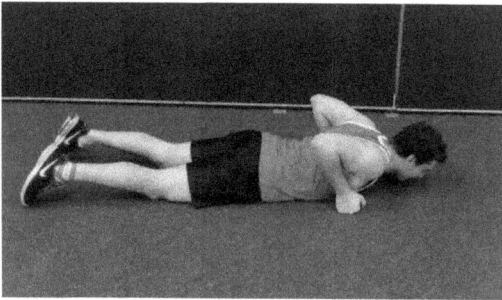

Step 1. Start by lying face down on the floor, then use your arms to push your upper body off the ground.
Step 2. Straighten your arms and push your pelvis into the floor until you get a good stretch through your midsection. Hold for 30-45 seconds.

The Side Cobra

(Obliques)

Same as the cobra, except you're focusing on your
oblique muscles. Start by lying on your side, then use
both hands to push your upper body off the floor so you
feel a stretch through your side. Hold for 20-30 seconds
and then repeat on opposite side.

The Kneeling Hip Flexor

(Abductors, obliques, quadriceps)

- Very effective for removing tightness through the hips and the front of the body.

Step 1. Start by placing one knee on a pillow or stretching mat, then bring other leg out with your foot flat on the ground.

Step 2. Make sure your pelvis/body remains facing forward and your front ankle remains under the knee. Try not to angle your thighs to either side – keep them in a straight line to the direction you're facing.

Step 3. Hold for 30-45 seconds.

This stretch can also be performed with an upper body twist or a raised rear leg for a better stretch (see over.)

The Pretzel
(Gluteus Maximus)

- Tricky, but great once you figure it out.

Step 1. Start by lying flat on your back with your right knee raised, and then bring left ankle onto right thigh.
Step 2. Lock in your left leg by gripping your right knee with your right hand, then using your left hand, reach under your left leg and grip your right shin.
Step 3. Feel the stretch through your left glute by pulling your right leg, while trying to rest your head on the floor. Hold for 30-45 secs then repeat on other leg.

Part 4: When you're in pain

Ready to pop a painkiller? Hang in there and have a read of these first.

LOWER BACK/HIPS

Lower back pain? Well it's probably because you've worked a long shift on your feet, walked around all day or you've been sitting down for too long. The consequence of these activities is compression in the lumber spine, which are the lowermost vertebrate of your back. When the lumbar spine compresses, it's not just a matter of the space between bones becoming smaller; the entire are moves forward. Because your lumber spine is naturally curved towards your belly button (see diagram), the curve will become more pronounced when weight pushes down on spine, and because your erector spinae muscles are trying to pull in back into line, they will seize up.

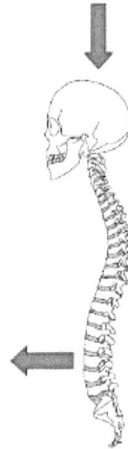

The solution: straighten and lengthen your lumbar spine.

The Legs on a Chair

The title may throw you, but this is in fact, when you put your legs on a chair. By lying in the position depicted here, you will bring your lumbar spine back into alignment.

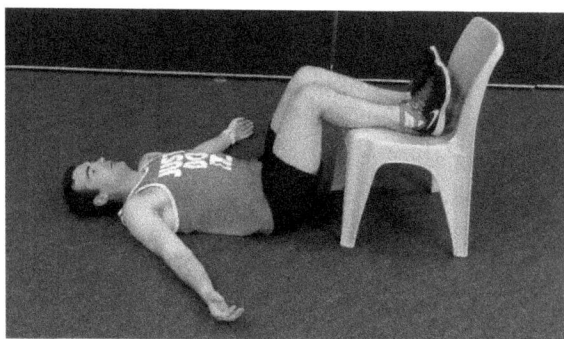

Step 1. Lie on the ground with your calves resting on a chair or sofa, pulling your hips in so your thighs and calves are at a 90 degree angle.

Step 2. Press your belly button to the floor, flattening your lumbar spine.

Step 3. Remain there for 5-10 mins.

Essentially, this position will straighten the curve in your lumbar spine, which will alleviate the lower back pain by allowing your erector spinae muscles to relax.

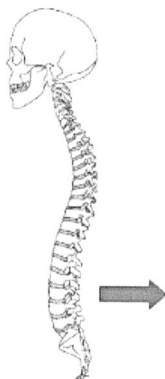

The Hangout
(Lumber spine)

- Simple, so so simple...

As you may be aware, gravity pulls you down all day and compresses your entire spine. By hanging from a safe structure with your feet off the ground for 20-30 seconds, you can relieve the force gravity has inflicted on you throughout the day. You may feel some tightness in your hips and lower back when you begin this exercise, but generally, it should not be painful. Stop if you are experiencing any shoulder or joint pain.

Alternatively, this exercise can also be performed with 'gravity boots', which enable you to hang upside-down and will give you a greater stretching/lengthening effect on your legs and hips. Gravity boots can be purchased from sport stores or the internet.

The Hip Fix
(Pelvis)

- "Omg", you'll say

This is the greatest stretch I've found so far, because it can cure back pain in literally 5 minutes. Because we sit down so much in awkward positions, especially with our legs angled into our pelvis, there is usually a lot of compression around the tailbone area. After a few hours of working, driving or sitting down, it is likely that your pelvis has been pulled forward and is in need of being pushed back and separated.

Step 1. Start by going down on all fours, then raise your right leg so that it makes a straight line with your upper body.

Step 2. Allow yourself to 'sink' into your supporting leg so that your pelvis is being pushed back and up into the air. This counteracts the pulling force a chair has on your hips. Hold for 30-45 seconds

Step 3. Bring your raised right leg down over your left knee, then move both hands about half a foot to the left. You should now be feeling a good stretch on the outside of your left thigh and through your pelvis. Hold for 30-45 seconds

Step 4. Repeat on the other side.

The Pelvic Click

(*Pelvis*)

Counteract the compression your tailbone receives on a daily basis.

Step 1. Lie on your back with legs raised off the ground and knees bent.

Step 2. Make two fists and hold them together between your knees.

Step 3. Push your knees together for 10-15 seconds. (you can sometimes hear a click, but that's nothing to worry about; a click is just trapped air escaping[2]).

NECK

If you find that you have a sore neck, it is very likely this strain is a result of tension built up in your legs and lower back. Performing the above exercises should help with most of the pain, but there are other exercises you can do to release the tension.

The Chin Tuck

(Neck, Shoulders, erector spinae, hamstrings, calves)

Stretch those muscles from your head to your toes.

Step 1. Bend over and grab the back of your head
Step 2. Pull your head down so that your chin touches your chest. Hold for 30-45 seconds.

The Cobra

See previous stretches in this section.

This stretch will counteract bad posture, relieving the stress placed on the front of the vertebrate in your neck. This may seem counterintuitive to relieving neck pain, but chances are your neck is cramping because you've been hunched over all day. By tightening, your muscles are trying to compensate for others, or trying to pull your spine in a certain direction to correct the overall shape. This position is doing the job for them.

Part 5: Long Term Maintenance

Strengthening Exercises

Strengthening exercises should begin once you've been stretching on a daily basis for a number of weeks and there is a noticeable improvement in your flexibility. If you perform strengthening exercises when you are cramping, there is a good chance you'll experience more pain due to the lactic acid buildup that results from exercising[2]. The best approach I've found to alleviating back pain is to manage the pain through stretching, then to strengthen your muscles whilst maintaining your newfound flexibility.

When you have progressed to the strengthening stage, perform dynamic stretching for 5-10 mins before you begin. This may be tedious and time-consuming, but the alternative is a neglected muscle system that does not function correctly. Remember: you can't work out certain parts of your body and neglect the rest, because this will leave you out of proportion and create a greater strain on surrounding muscle groups. The following exercises should be included in any full body gym routine, which is best prescribed to you by a personal trainer following an appraisal. Once again, if you have doubts as to how to perform an exercise, or feel one is not right for you, **consult a personal trainer**.

BRIDGES

Paul Wade, author of *Convict Conditioning* and calisthenics master, has this to say about bridging:

"If I had to name the most important strength building exercise in the world, it would be the bridge. Nothing else even comes close."

These exercises will:
- Help remove back pain caused by sitting down or standing all day
- Prepare the spine for heavy lifting movements, such as squats or deadlifts
- Strengthen muscles around the spine and reduce the likelihood of slipped discs
- Improve endurance for sport and everyday life

Front Bridge

Simple and effective.

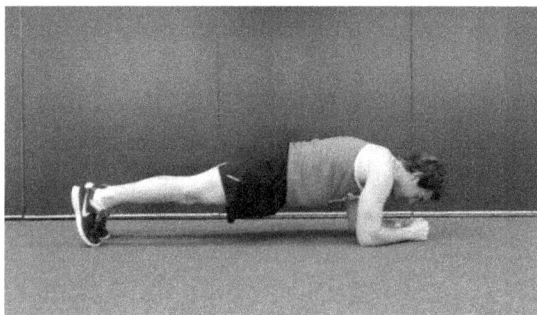

Step 1. Lie face down with your forearms parallel to each other.

Step 2. Raise up onto your toes and elbows, keeping your body in a straight line. Keep elbows under shoulders.

Step 3. Aim to hold for 30 seconds, then progress to 120 seconds.

Side Bridge

Same as the front bridge, but you're supporting yourself with one forearm and the using the side of the your foot. Hold for 30-120 seconds and repeat on opposite side.

Back Bridge

Great for building strength through the lower back and taking the strain off the abdominals.

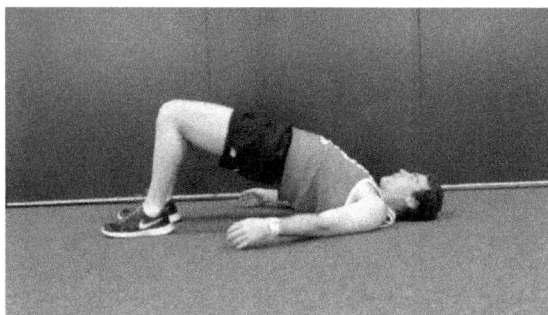

Step 1. Lie on your back with your hands flat on the ground and your feet tucked into your rear end.
Step 2. Push upwards through your hips, keeping your body straight from your chest to your knees.
Step 3. Hold for 30 -120 seconds.
Step 4. Repeat hold, but with one leg straight, then repeat for other leg. (These are be called single-legged bridges and require a lot of strength. Try and build up to a 30 second hold).

IN THE GYM

The following exercises should be performed in conjunction with a full body workout routine. Remember: if you only exercise certain parts of your body, you will leave some muscles developed and others under-developed, resulting in a disproportioned muscular system and you will increase your chances of injury[2].

Hyper extensions
(Hamstrings, glutes and erector spinae*)*

- Improves strength through lower back, hamstrings and glutes.

Step 1. Locate the 45 degree hyper extension station and find the correct position. Your hip bones should be just higher than the pads underneath your thighs.

Step 2. With your hands on your chest, lower yourself down slowly, then pull back up. Keep a straight line from your heels to your head and don't go any higher, otherwise you risk injury. You can also put your hands behind your head to increase the weight once you find the exercise too easy.

Step 3. Do 2-3 sets of 8-12 reps.

Swiss ball Hyper extensions

(Hamstrings, glutes and erector spinae*)*

A great exercise to strengthen the stabilizer muscles around your spinal cord.

Step 1. Place a Swiss Ball on top of a bench and lie on top of it with your hands gripping the bench.
Step 2. Keeping your legs straight, lower them toward the ground, then lift them back up to the starting position. Concentrate on isolating your lower back muscles.
Step 3. Do 2-3 sets of 8-12 reps.

Squats, deadlifts and upright rows

If you are at this stage, it means you have significantly increased your flexibility, you are relatively pain-free and you are ready to strengthen your body. Believe it or not, but lifting weight through your hips and back can be very effective when it comes to warding off back pain and remaining pain-free for a sustained period of time.

There are a number of exercises that can be performed to strengthen your back, all with different techniques and warm up exercises. Ideally, these exercises should be performed in a gym and the technique that is right for you should be demonstrated to you by a personal trainer. I recommend that you book an appraisal at your gym and learn the correct technique before lifting any weights.

REMEMBER: *Perform dynamic stretching before exercising and static stretching after your workout.*

Part 6: The other stuff

Orthotics

When I found physical treatment of my back pain unsuccessful, my mother suggested that I see a podiatrist to get my feet checked. "But it's my back... not my feet," I said naively, but after acquiring orthotics, I wish I'd found them sooner.. Within days, I could feel greater alignment through my spine and a significant reduction in back pain, and the more I thought about it, the more it made sense. Since your feet are bearing your entire body weight, it's very important that we look after them, and correct any problems that may be transferring up through the body.

What are they?

Orthotics are custom-made foot supports designed specifically for your feet and are placed inside your shoes. They are made of plastic, rubber or foam and prescribed to treat various disorders of the lower back, feet, ankles and legs. Simple inserts can be purchased from sports and department stores, however these are generic moulds and may not be provide you with the specific support you need. Custom-made orthotics are provided by a podiatrist and can be a few hundred dollars, but they can be worn for life and are a very good investment in your body and overall happiness.

Painkillers, Creams and Ointments

In addition to what you're ingesting, what gets absorbs through your skin will also affect the chemical processes that occur in your body. When it comes to muscular pain, I'm not the biggest fan of using heat rubs and ice gels for two main reasons:

1. They only provide a temporary solution to pain.
2. The majority of these products use potent chemicals are not naturally based.

If you are trying to overcome back pain, it makes more sense to invest your time, money and effort in something that will provide relief on a long-term basis, otherwise you will find yourself stuck in a rut. This means any reliance your body has built up for painkillers, creams and gels has to stop. Many people will testify that after they stop taking their migraine medication for a short period of time, their migraines finally go away, and the same principal applies to temporary solutions for back pain. If you're constantly taking painkillers or applying a gel product, it is possible for your body to 'bring on' the pain to get the hit of chemicals, which basically means you're becoming addicted.

As you are performing the exercises in the previous sections (on a daily basis), I recommend that you wane off the products/medications you are using so that you give your body the best chance to attain long-term relief of back pain.

The Foam Roller

An essential tool when it comes to relieving back and muscle pain. As the name implies, you literally roll yourself back on forth on the foam to massage your muscles. They are available from any sports store and they come in many shapes and sizes.

The best thing about the foam roller is it can be used to massage all the major muscle groups and are very effective when it comes to removing knots and loosening up the muscles. All the exercises you can do are available online following a quick search, but the best ones I've found are:

Upper to Lower Back

- Great for realigning the entire spine.

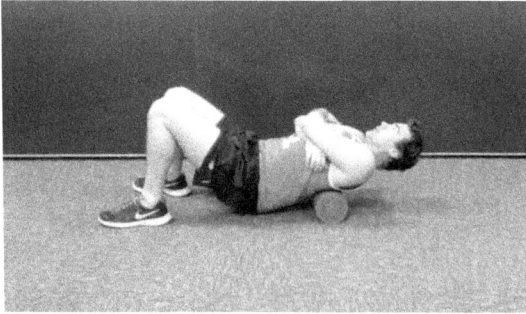

Step 1. Start by resting your upper back on top of the foam roller with your arms crossed over your chest, spreading out your back muscles as wide as you can.
Step 2. Use your legs to push yourself along the roller, all the way down to the base of your spine.
Step 3. Pull your legs to bring yourself back to the start position, then repeat the motion 5-10 times.

Glute Dip

Step 1. Place yourself on top of the foam roller, angling your body so your glute muscle is bearing your weight. Hold the same leg on your opposite thigh.

Step 2. By maintaining strength through your arms, legs and core, allow yourself to slide down the foam roller about 5-10 cm. You should feel a good push/massage on your glute.

Step 3. Pull through your body and bring yourself back to the starting position, then repeat 5-10 times. You can then perform the exercise on the opposite side.

Quad Roll

- Your quads are big, powerful muscles that you use a lot, so take care of them.

Step 1. Start by positioning yourself on the roller so that the top of your quadriceps muscle is bearing your weight. Support your upper body by resting on your forearms.
Step 2. Use your arms to push yourself down the roller, which will massage your quad.
Step 3. Return to the start position and repeat the motion 5-10 times. You can angle your body slightly to either side to generate more force on the knotted areas.

Hamstring Slide

Studies have shown that short, overworked hamstrings are related to lower back pain. Target these areas!

Step 1. Position yourself on top of the roller with the bottom of your hamstring supporting your weight.
Step 2. Use your arms and opposite leg to move down the roller, allowing your hamstring to take the upward force from the roller.
Step 3. Move back to the starting position, then repeat the motion 5-10 times. Repeat on opposite leg.

Calf Slide

This exact movement can also be performed on the calves:

Always Remember: Back pain can be a result of what is happening in your legs. Set aside time in your day for proper maintenance.

Part 7: Dos and Don'ts

- ## Do
    - Stretch everyday
    - Look after your diet
    - Stay hydrated
    - Keep hips and feet flat while sitting.
    - Dynamic stretching in the morning/before exercise
    - Static stretching after exercise/during the day/before sleeping
    - Believe pain can go away very quickly
    - Buy the best supportive mattress you can afford

- ## Don't
    - Wear heels (they instantly puts strain on your knees, hips, back and neck)
    - Cross legs while sitting.
    - Sit or stand for hours on end
    - Cause yourself any pain during stretching
    - Give up after a few days
    - Spend days on end in bed
    - Get involved in any high-speed Formula 1 accidents

References

1. Worrell T, Perrin D: Hamstring Muscle Injury: The Influence of Strength, Flexibility, Warm-Up, and Fatigue. *J Orthop Sports Phys Ther.* 1992, 16 (1)**:**12-18.

2. McArdle, W.D, Katch, F.I, & Katch, V.L (2010). *Exercise Physiology: Nutrition, Energy, and Human Performance*. Lippincott Williams & Wilkins, Philadelphia.

3. National Health and Medical Research Council (NHMRC). (2014) Nutrient reference values. Retrieved from www.nrv.gov.au.

4. Esola, M. A., McClure, P. W., Fitzgerald, G. K. & Siegler, S. (1996). Analysis of lumbar spine and hip motion during forward bending in subjects with and without a history of low back pain. *Spine*. *21*(1).

5. Yamaguchi, Taichi, Ishii & Kojiro. (2005). Effects of Static Stretching for 30 seconds and Dynamic Stretching on Leg Extension Power. *The Journal of Strength and Conditioning Research.* 19 (3).

6. McMillian D, Moore J, Hatler B & Taylor D (2006). Dynamic vs. Static-Stretching Warm Up: The Effect on Power and Agility Performance. *The Journal of Strength and Conditioning Research.* 20 (3).

7. Little T & Williams A. (2006). Effects of Differential Stretching Protocols During Warm-Ups on High-Speed

Motor Capacities in Professional Soccer Players. *The Journal of Strength and Conditioning Research.* 20 (1).

8. Cramer, J. T., Housh, T. J., Johnson, G. O., Miller, J. M., Coburn, J. W., & Beck, T. W. (2004). Acute effects of static stretching on peak torque in women. *The Journal of Strength & Conditioning Research.* 18(2).

9. Bandy, W.D, Irion, J.M. & Briggler M. (1998). The Effect of Static Stretch and Dynamic Range of Motion Training on the Flexibility of the Hamstring Muscles. *J Orthop Sports Phys Ther* 1998, 27(4).

10. Davis D.S., Ashby P.E., McCale K.L., McQuain J.A & Wine J.M. (2005). The Effectiveness of 3 Stretching Techniques on Hamstring Flexibility using Consistent Parameters. *Journal of Strength and Conditioning Research.* 19 (1).

11. De Weijer V,C, Gorniak G.C. & Shamus E. (2003). The Effect of Static Stretch and Warm-Up Exercise on Hamstring Length Over the Course of 24 Hours. *Journal of Orthopaedic Sports and Physical Therapy.* 33 (12).

www.ingramcontent.com/pod-product-compliance
Lightning Source LLC
LaVergne TN
LVHW051427080426
835508LV00022B/3279